Babel's Moon

Tupelo Press Snowbound Series Chapbook Award Winners

Barbara Tran, *In the Mynah Bird's Own Words*
Selected by Robert Wrigley

David Hernandez, *A House Waiting for Music*
Selected by Ray Gonzalez

Mark Yakich, *The Making of Collateral Beauty*
Selected by Mary Ruefle

Joy Katz, *The Garden Room*
Selected by Lisa Russ Spaar

Cecilia Woloch, *Narcissus*
Selected by Marie Howe

John Cross, *staring at the animal*
Selected by Gillian Conoley

Stacey Waite, *the lake has no saint*
Selected by Dana Levin

Brandon Som, *Babel's Moon*
Selected by Aimee Nezhukumatathil

Babel's Moon

Brandon Som

Poems

TUPELO PRESS
NORTH ADAMS, MASSACHUSETTS

Babel's Moon.
Copyright 2011 Brandon Som. All rights reserved.
ISBN-13: 978-1-936797-04-2

Cover and text designed by Bill Kuch, WK Graphic Design.

First paperback edition: November 2011.

Tupelo Press is an award-winning independent literary press that
publishes fine fiction, nonfiction, and poetry in books that are a joy
to hold as well as read. Tupelo Press is a registered 501(c)3 nonprofit
organization and relies on donations to carry out its mission of
publishing extraordinary work that may be outside the realm of large
commercial publishers.

NATIONAL
ENDOWMENT
FOR THE ARTS

Supported in part by an award from
the National Endowment for the Arts

Yow Choy Som 1914–1994

Contents

Babel's Moon

Elegy

Of Babel's moon, I have notes. It was a marked card. It lit a chandelier out of an acacia. The trowel glinted with it. Crickets were out, too, and, as if they sightread stars, settled in to leg-kick song. A light wind blew seed into the web between tines of a hayrake. A soldier stood letting his horse drink well water from his helmet. The moon trembled there. There was nothing forsaken about it. It simply issued a shadow while burnishing a surface. This morning, I read that when returning from a trail, Thoreau knew he had had visitors by what was left behind: *a wreath of evergreen, a name in pencil on a walnut leaf, a willow wand woven into a ring.* Its path not without disruption, the moon, in its orbit, tethers and tethers again. The morning of the funeral, my father dressed my grandfather: from the eyelet, each button new to full; the tie's knot loose as if it had swallowed a small bird.

Tea

1

The limned moon nightly, an onion spinning,
but backward, rind to core, into existence,
has clicked counterclockwise. I spent the day
reading about Chinese tea—*dragon's well,*
orchid snow, left-by-birds—and the tea girls
in mountain villages who clip young buds
of flowers, extravagances that steal
the nutrient from the leaves they harvest
before the spring rains, when they are tender,
fragrant, close in size to a *sparrow's tongue.*

2

This morning in the stone cistern, spring melt
and yesterday's showers, one maple leaf,
russet, arthritic, stem thin as a riven
wishbone, a rethinking of the last thought
of autumn. Legend has it, tea was given
to China by the Bodhidharma, who,
wishing the prolonged states of wakefulness,
cut off each eyelid with harvest shears,
and where they fell a tea tree grew, each leaf,
shapes of the seed, the design of the sieve.

3

A sigh is sound-byte from the larger sough
in the trees, a re-recording attuned
to courting something higher than ourselves.
Because the rarer tea leaves in purer air
are accessible only to birds, magpies,
it is widely believed, have built their nests
with the finest and most fragrant of tea.
It has been said that some will hunt the bird
returning to roost and carrying by beak
or by its talons just one or two leaves.

If St. Augustine Were a Butcher
Like My Grandfather

He would walk into the meat locker
where the side of steer hung
from chains—the red meats separated
by white fats, lucent as candle
wax—and begin sharpening, cleaver
to rod, getting the blade down
to the fine edge where steel tapers
into nothing and so can tend
to flesh. The metals' high pitch would
sound like mice in the garnet sacks
of feed, while the coops behind
the market were silent, and the dogs
asleep, well fed on the stomach
of a sow. In the cooler, his breath
would leave his mouth in small clouds,
as he made the first cuts in the hind
quarters, carving out the roasts,
and later moved just behind the ribs
for the steaks he'd flense of gristle
and membrane, pausing at times
to push back, with his wrist, his wire-
rimmed glasses that continually slipped,
or to wipe bloodwet hands and add
to the apron more of his fingerprints.
As morning came and lit outside

the freeway, he would bone and trim
the forequarters, running the chuck
through the grinder before placing
the cuts, priced by the pound, behind
the glass and switching on the light
so the red in the raw meats glowed.

The Nest Collectors

Then the circuit tripped, and under alley stars
above the breaker box, I found the twig nest
with bits of hatchling shell. I considered the one-
note hum one's home makes, the murmur
of watt and want the nestlings fledged above,
forming their own warble from need-cry. Once
at a wedding's banquet, my father, so often frugal,
spoke on the extravagance of the first course,
of the trellises, in sea caves in China, centuries-old
and twine-tethered by nest collectors. Shouldering
gunnysacks damp with spindrift, they forage
the swift nests for the blood-spittle that binds twig
to twig and is a delicacy seasoning a soup's broth.
I looked for what bound my nest but found
nothing for profit or to pawn, though in my hand
it was round as a pocketwatch—a pocketwatch
with fob that once tethered a bird. Mason of the avian,
father said, sipping from his Seven and Seven.
Then the sea bass came with slivers of scallion.
We used our soup bowls, discreetly, for the bones.

Jesus was fond of knock-knock jokes and not so much wine, except maybe wine made from certain flowers, lilac or dandelion. It is virtuous to say what you mean, which would suggest what you mean is always waiting to be announced, the way the archangel Gabriel came to Mary, nervous, as I understand it, with the task of announcing the birth of the baby Jesus. We say *come out with it, come clean* because meaning, like Mary, is pregnant, labored; and immaculate conception is, in some sense, coming clean in such a way that it doesn't get around, that it is kept quiet or maybe just kept between angels. As I understand it, Jesus one evening came upon two girls catching crickets by lanterns. They were telling knock-knock jokes. It was April, so they had blossoms, lilac or dandelion, stuck to the bottoms of their bare feet. And the angels, who always have something to say, and a quiet despair for the things they have to say, which is why they are angels, were now silent in the limbs of an olive tree watching Jesus tell his knock-knock joke to two girls, who asked, in unison, and without hesitation, *who's there?*

The Sawhorses

Because of something I didn't get
right with someone, I look up
at what the sky pulls off,
only to approach those sawhorses
still standing from my last
effortless segue, and their presence
points to something precarious
like the single star
I've chosen as the linchpin
for all the stars. These evenings
teleprompt: the rays of light slipping
into the dark well of a period
and so the end of another
thought. Like this moon
carrying the dark vestiges
of its former selves, we are defined
in these moments of difference.
Prior to the light bulb,
candlelight rarely set the mood,
and the self, too, is a technology
patented, at times outdated and obsolete
as the belly button—that tin
can and string hooked up to starlight.

Sugimoto

Of the horizon we know
Very little up close and figure
The intent as a streamlining
Of our own inarticulate selves.
Recently, I had the opportunity
To hold one in my hands. Let me
Underscore its resistance to form.
My fingers felt as if thousands
Of miles were between them.

Then they moved to the sea.
At the beach they let go
The kite string and the sky
Before them seemed even more
Immense and yet still
Leaning on those instances
That added up to the present
Sackcloth of clouds and wind
Assailing, suddenly all shoulders.

The story of the bird is a girl
In a devout grief against a sea
That eddies because its memory
Of the sky is at once collective
And dissipating as it becomes
Sky again. The plan was simple:
Fathom both grief and sea
With stones displacing each
The way a wing does the wind.

Underground disorients us
From above which explains why
We've forgotten so much of heaven.
A subway car sounds like you
Searching the silverware
For a tablespoon, while tunnels turn
The windows of the train to mirrors
Because the opaque, in its refusing
Of the light, affords us reflection.

They say in certain shells
You still hear the sea.
What urgency is there still
Left in such long-distant
Phone calls in which the past
Is in our hands by some
Rendering tinged with loss:
The sea in desperate karaoke
Disarmingly maudlin in mono.

After this, bridges followed him
Home, shirking responsibility, so
The city was hamstrung. Telling him
Similar dreams of sawing men
In half, they approached the sympathies
That have made them the outbursts
Of our solitudes. Seeing something
Of himself, he watched them return
To tender themselves at dawn.

The essential idiom of the sea
Comes to terms in the calligraphic
Coast. Sea brought, kelp dries
In the sunlight on the shore rocks.
Day is a hogtying, a stark light
Drying them out, so she fished
From her day bag a tin of bee balm.
And the tide had its slipknot
And the day moon its oarlock.

Overtime, my lips were a kite
Tied off at the back of my throat.
Hers were a beak evolved
From a diet of settling a score.
Godlike, the sea swallowed
For the sake of form. Awe occurs
When we can't measure certain
Distances, while our mouths open,
As if to challenge with our own immensity.

Among the ideal forms
Complete and hung past the veils
And valences of the night's sky
He liked those which explained away
His finding the old answering
Machine with its tape still spooled
And cued: she'd be late. These nights
He put a book down. He walked away.
Ellipses trailed him to the other room.

Ocotillo

Torch and Coachwhip: one to see by,
          one to lead with. Even so, the branches
seemed to suture some wound between
          the land and sky directly behind them,

their splay the long hair of my mother
          as she jumped, feet-first, into the summer
pool for her night swim—their Nauhtl name
          extinguishing in the gathering dusk.

Spring months, hummingbirds came
          with their great thirst, hovered and buried
their heads in the red-flushed flutes:
          tenderness there despite the thorns (or

is it because) and adornment, too, to more
          easily seduce—a lover offering each
polished nail to suck. How little the wind
          wants to do with it, and how little shade

it offers: unable to indulge more of itself,
          even shadow, it thins—leaves, spendthrift,
like the wet footprints of my mother—
          small, dark birds the heat will gather

from flagstone steps, while past the fence
          and root-tethered, these harps of rebar,
pizzicato, play out two kinds of forgetting:
          one consumed by desire, one released from it.

In the house two boys undress in front of each other and find wind chimes where their genitalia should be. So one boy gets down on his knees and blows on them. A few clouds go by the windows earning their inconsistencies, and in the room some dresser drawers are open like balconies over a small parade. There is a print above them by the Japanese artist Utamaro, in which two teahouse girls are dressing their hair before their mirrors in the morning. You can see one's knee, and this is enough to know they are alone and unaware of us watching as one pulls a whale bone comb through her hair, and the other fixes the knot of her ribbon, both with hands that later might cover a smile. But this moment is before the customers in the early light of the pleasure quarter, before the traffic of gamblers and courtesans. It is a moment in an affair with essence, as two women stare in separate mirrors and begin to pin their hair like the wings of intricate insects. In this moment with themselves and themselves in their mirrors, the artist has fastened a moment without so much as a tremble, so still that even now we might imagine one placing her hands in her own reflection like water for laundry and then suddenly throwing it out and startling a dog asleep in the alley.

My Grandfather in the Lemon Orchard

1

Without mouths
trees house birds, wait
on wind for susurrant leaves.
In Northern California
you have a mouth of leaves
and birds, in an orchard
where you hood and bud
until bloom. Years
in the mouth quill and alight
between us now, so I go,
with a ladder, my arm
through the rungs,
shouldering its length,
past the burdened crowns,
twisted bramble, where drunk
orchard birds, in some explanation
of carpentry, come
like books, winged jackets
and foxed flyleaves,
returned to their shelves.

2

When he kisses her in the lemon orchard
the stars come out to stitch a wound.
There are wells beneath the trees
as if the trees are standing in the black
dresses they've just slipped off.
She's still wearing hers and it has a bow
like two or three butterflies
feeding on poppies.

They don't know
what they deserve and so don't say
their names. A few birds return to the trees
to bite their backs for lice. They don't know
what to do with their hands, so the stars come
out to work in the fields. They can hear
the harness slipping from the horse
beside the canal where dragonflies settle
and draw moons around themselves.

3

Swaddled in limb sap,
I imagine myself, impulse,
a cadence, a prevailing hunger
or thirst to avail myself of the light
and blister. Addled by divisions,
finding myself in pieces, I am nonetheless
driven, and as waves swell
or clouds congress before they burst,
I am under the enchantment of a single mind,
overwhelmed with the forgetting
that prepares me and ushers me
to form, while around me so much
is zipped—a kit bag—closed.
And I am, finally, a coin in its purse,
a seed sealed in its pulp.

4

I wanted to be the lather brush
in my grandfather's kit bag
bristled and smelling of the bay rum
he bought in cakes and kept
in a mug and sudsed his face with
before taking the straight razor
to his cheek, jaw, and neck to impress
his bride overseas with this photo
in which he stands beside
a borrowed bicycle and wears
his wire-rimmed glasses and one
good suit. Belonging, its *longing*'s
root in the tongue—that grub
in the mouth's dark loam—ravels
in what we save up to say.
I think of their words but don't know
the tongue, and knuckle in dumb and wait.

5

The ladder makes a gunwale
he rudders through the orchard
until its prow upends and noses

into the limbs of the trees.
I like to think of him, a thought
engrossed in the crown—another

kind of thought—of a tree,
so easily distracted by particulars:
this ladder, this man, a robin alight

with grub unlaced in its mouth.
In the one mole on his temple
a horse kicked up hooves. Of desire,

I know to bring it out is to burden
the base and limb of the tree, to await
the shape of the season's crop.

A sign of good business sense
and virility the Chinese say, the mole
had done away with his hair

by the time I was born. I like to think
of it all those years, in hiding,
a landmine, a blackbird in tall grass.

Alba: The Archer Yi

Because we are helpless in the affairs
of heaven, we place feathers on arrows.
By dowel, the nock's groove against
its bowstring, the arrow by bird's wing,
by archer's sight, by aim, superimposing
what is in hand over what is distant,
we arrive at certain conclusions, the end
of this tale for example: after blight
and the consequent famine, nine of ten
suns fell as dark crows. Of the ways
it is told, there's the account of the emperor,
as the ninth sun lay writhing—dark blood
on dark feathers—placing his hand on
the archer's shoulder, so the slung bow
was lowered, a discretion, the story would
have us believe, that is, finally, this sun,
this light, still with its obsession to travel
while we go on living in its obstruction,
even now, this morning, your shoulder white
as scrimshaw, drawing the light to its fletching.

Noche Buena

Before another rasp-worked moon, I'll tender a clutch of cardinals, or the flush on a runner's cheek, to better render the young girl's gift to the Christ-child. Flame Leaf. Star Flower. What is evening in evening? By what accounting? The sky will go away despite the trees thrashing and the smoke giving chase from the chimneys. "Too much torn to make a drawing," Audubon wrote of a hermit thrush after the day's hunt. Isn't it also true of some stories? The infinite graftings. Here, you take a cutting. The blood-colored leaf, once over the heart, was thought to increase circulation. Ingested, it was believed to reduce fever. You might, however, place it in the pages of a breviary beside a favorite psalm.

Notes

The sequence "Sugimoto" works from the series *Seascapes* by the photographer Hiroshi Sugimoto.

"Tea" borrows from the book *The Chinese Art of Tea* by John Blofeld (Shambhala, 1997).

Acknowledgments

Grateful acknowledgment to the editors of the journals in which the following poems first appeared, sometimes in earlier versions:

West Branch
"Corrido for Indiscretion," which is now a section of "My Grandfather in the Lemon Orchard"

Octopus Magazine
"Sugimoto"

"Identity Poem" was chosen for the anthology *The McSweeney's Book of Poets Picking Poets* (Dominic Luxford, curator; McSweeney's Books, 2007).

"Alba: The Archer Yi" was chosen for the anthology *Best New Poets 2007* (Natasha Trethewey and John Livingood, editors; University of Virginia Press, 2007).

Other books from Tupelo Press

Fasting for Ramadan, Kazim Ali
This Lamentable City, Polina Barskova,
edited and introduced by Ilya Kaminsky
Circle's Apprentice, Dan Beachy-Quick
Cloisters, Kristin Bock
Stone Lyre: Poems of René Char,
translated by Nancy Naomi Carlson
Poor-Mouth Jubilee, Michael Chitwood
Severance Songs, Joshua Corey
Atlas Hour, Carol Ann Davis
Sanderlings, Geri Doran
The Flight Cage, Rebecca Dunham
Then, Something, Patricia Fargnoli
The Posthumous Affair, James Friel
Have, Marc Gaba
Other Fugitives & Other Strangers, Rigoberto González
Red Summer, Amaud Jamaul Johnson
Dancing in Odessa, Ilya Kaminsky
Manoleria, Daniel Khalastchi
Ardor, Karen An-hwei Lee
Biogeography, Sandra Meek
Flinch of Song, Jennifer Militello
Lucky Fish, Aimee Nezhukumatathil
Intimate, Paisley Rekdal
The Forest of Sure Things, Megan Snyder-Camp
Human Nature, Gary Soto
Traffic with Macbeth, Larissa Szporluk
Archicembalo, G. C. Waldrep
Dogged Hearts, Ellen Doré Watson
Monkey Lightning, Martha Zweig

See our complete backlist at www.tupelopress.org